Changing Cultures

Jan Anderson

Harcourt Achieve

Rigby • Saxon • Steck-Vaughn

www.HarcourtAchieve.com
1.800.531.5015

PM Extras Non-Fiction
Ruby Level 27

U.S. Edition © 2013 HMH Supplemental Publishers
10801 N. MoPac Expressway
Building #3
Austin, TX 78759
www.hmhsupplemental.com

Text © 2004 Cengage Learning Australia Pty Limited
Illustrations © 2004 Cengage Learning Australia Pty Limited
Originally published in Australia by Cengage Learning Australia

8   1957   15
4500544468

Text: Jan Anderson
Printed in China by 1010 Printing International Ltd

Acknowledgments
The author and publisher would like to acknowledge permission to reproduce material from the following sources:
Photographs by AAP Image/AFP/Timothy Clary, p. 22 top /Top Cole, p. 23 bottom;Austral International/Stock Food, pp. 9, 12 top; Australian Picture Library, p. 26; Australian Picture Library/Corbis, pp. 7 bottom, 16 bottom right, 23 top /Ludo Kuipers, front cover top left, p 19 /Galen Rowell, front cover top right, p. 21 top /Brian A. Wikander, front cover bottom left, p. 15 bottom left /Galen Rowell, back cover /Catherin Karnow, p. 8 bottom /David Lees, p, 12bottom /Horan Tom, p. 13/Paul Barton, p. 14 /Jan Butchofsky-Houser, p. 15 top /Adam Woolfitt, p. 16 top left /Judy Griesedieck, p. 16 bottom left /Peter M. Wilson, p. 17 top right /Joyce Choo, p. 18 right /Clay Perry, p. 25 top right /Jim Cumminsl Era Publications for the photograph on p. 29 and extract pp. 29, 30 adapted from MARIA DONATO; When I was Youngl Copyright (c) 1996, Janeen Brian. First Published by Era Publications, Australia; Imagen/Bill Thomas, p.5 top; Lochman Transparancies, p. 7 top; Lonely Planet Images, pp. 4 bottom left, 11 top, 17 top left; Newspix, pp. 27 top & bottom, 28; Nokia, p. 4 bottom right; Photo Japan, p. 8 top; Photo New Zealand, p. 24 bottom left / Sarah Masters, p. 24 bottom right; Photodisc, p. 6 top; PhotoEdit/Marie Kate Denny, front cover bottom right, p.20 top; Photolibrary.com/Foodpix, p.6 bottom /Rick Sherwin, p. 15 bottom right /SuperStock, p. 24 top right; Phtos.com, p. 20 bottoml Stock Photos/Masterfile, p, 21 bottom, p. 24 top left, p. 25 top left.

Changing Cultures
ISBN 978 0 75 789236 3

Contents

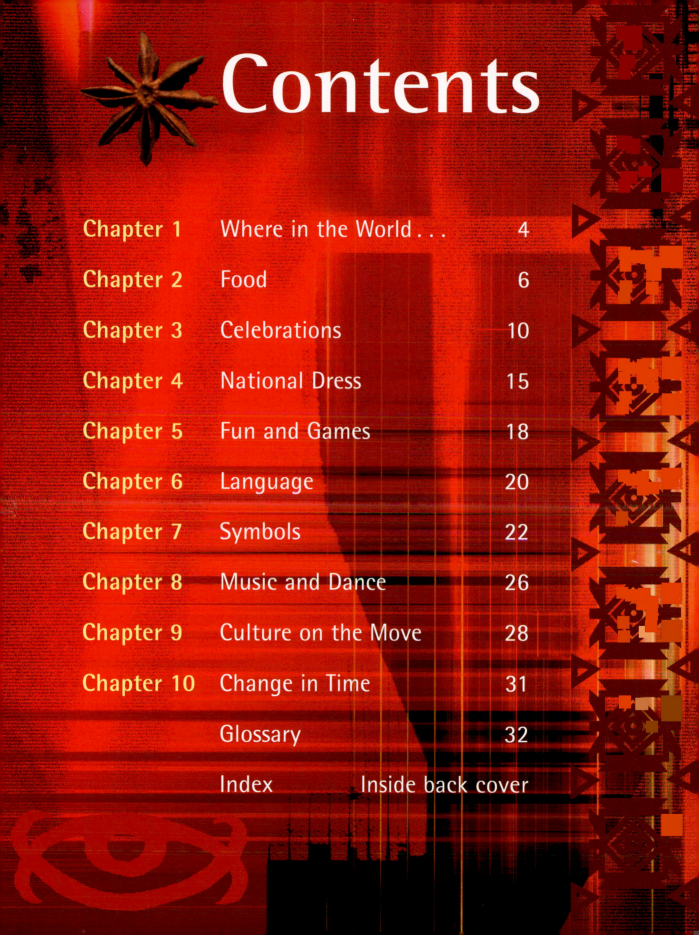

CHAPTER 1

Where in the World ...

Many of us were born in another country, or have parents and family who come from another part of the world. As both people and products move around the world, they bring far-away cultures closer together.

At home we cook with spices from India, at work we use mobile phones perhaps from Finland, and at school there are computers made in Japan or the United States of America.

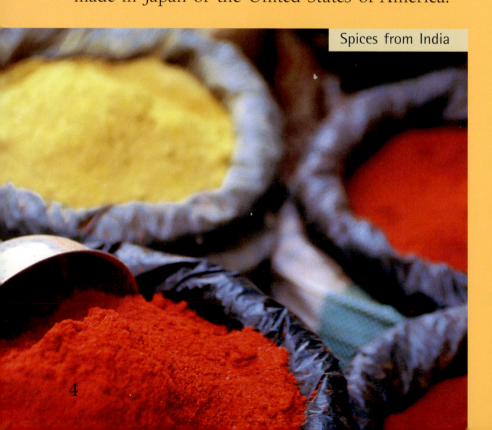

Spices from India

4

Learning about other cultures allows us to discover new ways of doing things. We can listen to different kinds of music and enjoy original foods.

We don't have to travel too far. We can explore almost every corner of the globe by using the internet. At the click of a button, we can be **virtual travelers,** and find out about cultures in many parts of the world that we've never even seen!

CHAPTER 2

Food

When people **migrate** from one country to another, they often take their recipes and cooking styles with them. Sometimes these migrants, or new settlers, start restaurants. So people living in Paris, New York, or Sydney can enjoy the foods of many different cultures all in the one place.

Traditionally one of Britain's national dishes was roast beef and Yorkshire pudding, but today, an Indian chicken tikka masala is just as common!

Quandongs

Bush tucker

In Australia bush **tucker**, or food that has been used by Aborigines for centuries, is now included in some modern Australian recipes.

Quandongs (said kwon-dongs) are a kind of native Australian fruit. They can be dried and preserved for later. Quandongs taste like apricots and can be made into a sweet pie.

Wattle seed

Wattle seed is now used in some Australian breads and biscuits. Qantas – the Australian national airline – has served wattle seed bread rolls with meals.

The Japanese Tea Ceremony

The Japanese tea **ceremony** is a tradition that is 800 years old. The ceremony, which can take some time, is meant to calm the guests and help them enjoy their surroundings. Some Japanese houses even have a special "tea room."

The surroundings for the tea ceremony are important. There is usually a scroll on the wall and a vase of flowers. These would have been specially chosen for the occasion. Tea ceremonies might be held to celebrate the blossoming of the cherry trees in spring or a get-together of friends.

A tea master serving tea

kettle

container of
powdered green tea

water ladle
made of
bamboo

stove for
heating
the water

tea bowls for
drinking

tea scoop

bamboo tea whisk

Guests kneel on a mat called a "tatami" (said tah-*tar*-me).
They are served by the "tea master," who has studied how
to conduct tea ceremonies. The tea master uses a scoop
to put some powdered green tea into the tea bowl.
Hot water is ladled in. The tea is whisked, which
makes it frothy. Sweets are served with the tea, because
green tea can taste bitter.

CHAPTER 3

Celebrations

New Year is an important time in many cultures. The date on which it is celebrated varies from culture to culture. Holiday customs and traditions also vary a lot from culture to culture.

New Year in Scotland

In Scotland people celebrate the coming of the new year with a big party on New Year's Eve, December 31. Scots call this celebration "Hogmanay."

In order to receive good luck in the new year, the first person to enter a Scottish home after midnight must be a black-haired man. He brings with him a piece of coal for the fire, which symbolizes warmth for the house in the coming year. He also has some traditional Scottish food, such as **black bun,** to represent plenty of food. And under his arm he carries something to drink. Everyone sings 'Auld Lang Syne' – a traditional Scottish song celebrating the importance of old friends.

This man is known as your "first foot" because he's the first person to put his foot across your doorway in the new year.

Chinese 'couplet' sayings on red paper

The Chinese New Year Festival

New Year in Western cultures can be a lively celebration that lasts from New Year's Eve to New Year's Day, but the Chinese New Year **Festival** can last from five days to three weeks!

Decorations are an important part of Chinese New Year. People hang "couplets" on walls and in doorways at home. These are good-luck sayings written on pieces of red paper.

Dinner on Chinese New Year's Eve is the most important meal of the year, because it's when the whole family gets together. The foods that are eaten are symbols of success and abundance for the following year. A whole fish or a whole chicken is considered lucky.

On New Year's Eve, family members give each other money in red envelopes. This is called "lucky money," because it symbolizes having money during the coming year.

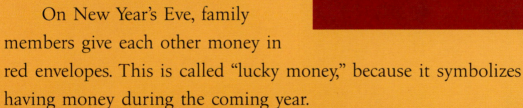

Did you know?

Chinese New Year begins at a different time every year. For example, in 2002 Chinese New Year started on February 12, but in 2003 the date was February 1.

A traditional panettone

An Italian Celebration

In December Italians like to eat special foods such as "panettone" (said pan-uh-*toe*-nay). These are cakes with sultanas and candied fruit inside them. One hundred years ago, traditional panettone were small and round and packed in drum-shaped boxes. Today they are tall and packed in square-shaped boxes. The modern panettone boxes are now famous around the world.

In Italy strolling musicians called "zampognari" play traditional holiday songs in the streets, using bagpipes, flutes, and oboes.

"Tet" Vietnamese New Year

In Vietnam preparations for the first day of the New Year, called Tet, take place for over a week. In many countries, the New Year begins on January 1, following the solar calendar. In other countries, such as Vietnam, it follows the lunar (moon) calendar and can begin anytime between the end of January and the middle of February.

The peach tree blsossoms are a sign of spring.

Tet is the most important holiday for the Vietnamese. Preparations include thorough house cleaning, the purchase of new clothes and shoes, the giving of gifts to family and friends, and decorating their homes and offices. One type of decoration is the peach tree in full bloom. The lacy, pink blossoms are a sign of the coming spring. The peach trees are sold in the markets, and then they are placed in homes, offices, and storefronts.

People buy peach trees to decorate their homes and businesses.

13

Thanksgiving Day

Thanksgiving is an American celebration that is centuries old. It began when the pilgrims gave thanks for the harvest and for having enough food to survive the upcoming winter.

The original Thanksgiving included the Native Americans who had helped the pilgrims settle and raise crops.

The traditional Thanksgiving meal includes turkey, stuffing, sweet potatoes, and pumpkin pie for dessert.

Did you know?

Thanksgiving Day in the United States is held on the fourth Thursday in November, whereas in Canada people celebrate on the second Monday in October.

CHAPTER 4

National Dress

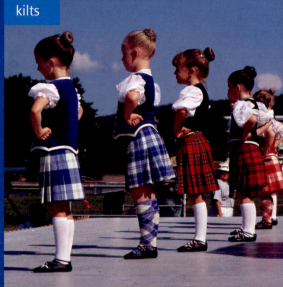

kilts

Throughout the world, there are many cultures that have a traditional dress, or costume. There is the bold tartan kilt in Scotland, the richly-colored sari in India, and the beautiful sarong in Indonesia.

Different kinds of clothing were produced to suit different climates, and they were made of materials that were easily obtained.

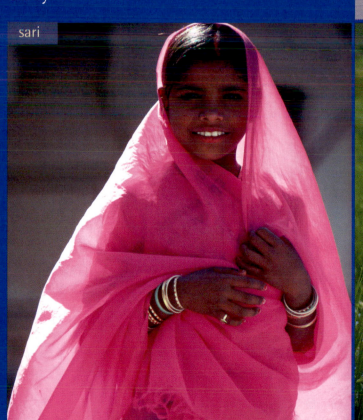

sari

sarongs

15

The Scottish kilt

The kilt is like a skirt. The first kilts were much bigger than those worn today, and could be taken off and used as a blanket at night. It must have been very handy in cold Scottish winters!

Today kilts in Scotland are mainly kept for special occasions like weddings and traditional celebrations. There are up to eight yards of material in every kilt, making them quite heavy to wear.

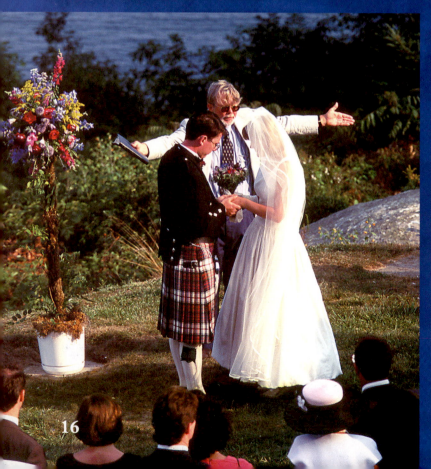

The Japanese kimono

The word "kimono" is Japanese for "a thing to wear." It is a long, loose piece of clothing with wide sleeves. It is tied with a wide sash, or belt, called an "obi." Kimonos don't have pockets, so a small wooden box, called an "inro," can be attached to the obi and used to carry things.

Today Japanese women wear the kimono for special occasions such as **graduations** or weddings, or for traditional ceremonies.

CHAPTER 5

Fun and Games

Today children who live in cultures with modern technology can play games on computers. Hand-held electronic games are also popular. Like computers, they have silicon chips inside them to make them work.

In the past, children played simple games, often using materials that they could find easily around them.

Knucklebones was a game that was played in Italy. It was played with small round pebbles. The game was called knucklebones because you had to throw the pebbles in the air, and catch them on the back of your hand, on your knuckles.

jacks

The same game was also played in Australia and Britain, where children called it jacks. As time passed, the jacks were made from brightly coloured plastic, and were all exactly the same shape.

Another game played in many different cultures was rolling a hoop. Old-fashioned hoops were made of steel or wood. Today hoops are plastic. Some children like swinging them around their waist.

Hopscotch

The game of hopscotch began in ancient Britain. Soldiers practiced their precise footwork on courts that were 100 feet long! Children imitated the soldiers and added a scoring system, using stones as the markers.

Today children all over the world play hopscotch on school playgrounds, on sidewalks, or any safe place they can find. Hopscotch has many names throughout the world, such as "Marselles" in France, "Templehupfen" in Germany, "Ekaria Dukaria" in India . . . but no matter what the name, hopscotch is a much enjoyed game by all children.

CHAPTER 6

Language

Words and language are an important part of any culture. People use language to communicate with each other. Even when people speak the same language, such as English, they use words differently, depending on where they live.

Proverbs and sayings can reveal a lot about a culture. "He who hesitates is lost" is an Australian proverb. "To a quick question, give a slow answer" is an Italian proverb. So in Australian culture, people seem to think it's best to act quickly, whereas in the Italian culture the opposite is thought to be better.

Even when a proverb means the same thing, it may consist of different words. For example, to avoid bad luck, Americans say "knock on wood," whereas Australians say "touch wood" and Italians say "touch iron!"

Did you know?

Universal signs like these three are understood by everyone. That is very handy when you are traveling and need to find the bathroom!

Language links

Different cultures take words from other languages. "Anorak" is an Eskimo word for a short coat with a hood that protects you from wind, rain, or cold. "Parka" is another Eskimo word that was used to describe an anorak with a fur-lined hood.

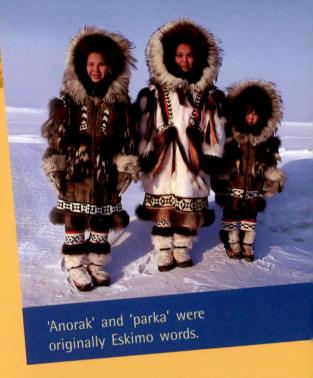

'Anorak' and 'parka' were originally Eskimo words.

English-speakers use the French word "gourmet" to describe someone who knows a lot about food.

Another word used in English is "pow-wow" – meaning "to get together for a chat, or discussion." It comes from a similar-sounding word used by some Native American tribes.

Did you know?

Over 3,000 languages will disappear this century as many cultures stop speaking their own language and use English or Chinese, instead.

"Kiosk" is often used to describe a small shop that is open at the front, and sells newspapers, sandwiches, and drinks. It comes from the Turkish word for "a pavilion," which is "kiusk."

The word "kiosk" comes from Turkey.

CHAPTER 7

Symbols

The symbols of a country are usually its flag, a **coat of arms,** and **emblems,** such as plants or animals.

Flags

The first flags were designed hundreds of years ago. Flags are used to represent a country, and unite the many cultures living there. Some flags are designed to reflect the history of a country. For example, the flag of the United States of America has 50 stars representing the number of states today. It also has 13 red and white stripes, which stand for the original colonies from which the country grew.

At the opening ceremony of the Olympic Games, teams from different countries are led by their flag-bearer. Although a flag is a simple rectangle of colored cloth, at an international event it becomes a powerful symbol of a country or national team.

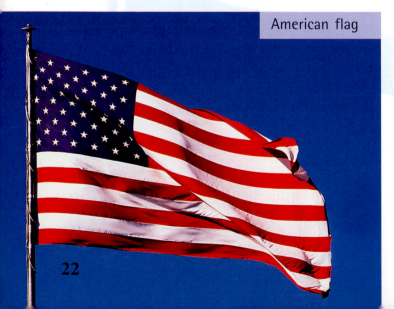

American flag

Did you know?

There were nine different designs of the American flag prior to the current design. The designs changed over time to reflect the growth of the United States of America.

Coats of arms

A coat of arms is a cultural symbol that is used by governments on buildings, and in official documents like passports.

On the American coat of arms, the American bald eagle is carrying a scroll with the motto "E Pluribus Unum." These Latin words mean "Out of many, one," because America, like many countries today, was formed from several cultures living in the one place.

THE GREAT SEAL OF THE UNITED STATES

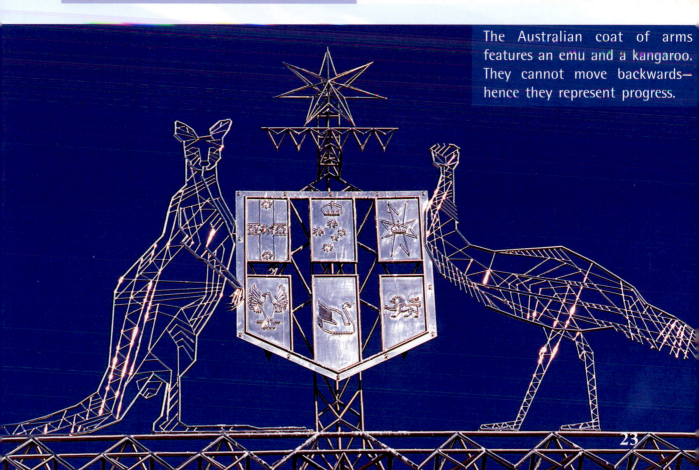

The Australian coat of arms features an emu and a kangaroo. They cannot move backwards—hence they represent progress.

23

National emblems

Native plants or animals are often used as the symbols, or emblems, of a country.

Canada

maple leaf

beaver

Mexico

eagle with snake

cactus

Scotland

thistle

England

rose

Australia

golden wattle

25

Music and Dance

Music and dance are an important part of many cultures. Crow Fair is a Native-American Pow-Wow where thousands of people enjoy dances, drumming, traditional ceremonies, and much more, annually.

Did you know?

Crow Fair has been held for over 100 years in the same location – near Custer's Last Stand battlegrounds, in Montana. Crow Fair's slogan is "Tee Pee Capital of the World."

Many Native Americans wear their traditional dress or "regalia" for the fair.

Mexican dancers wear very fancy skirts and blouses.

Mexicans celebrate their country's independence twice each year. Cinco de Mayo (The Fifth of May) commemorates Mexico's victory at the Battle of Puebla (1862). This holiday is vigorously celebrated in the Mexico state of Puebla and enthusiastically enjoyed in many other places, including in the U.S.

Mexican culture is the focus of Cinco de Mayo. Traditional food, music, dances, and customs are appreciated by everyone who joins in the festivities.

Traditional dances are performed during Kwanzaa.

Did you know?

Kwanzaa is an African-American holiday that focuses on the traditional African values of family, community, commerce, and self-improvement. Seven principles (Nguzo Saba) are observed from December 26 to January 1st.

27

CHAPTER 9

Culture on the Move

When people migrate from one country to another, they sometimes continue doing the things they enjoyed doing in the country or culture from which they came. An example of this is the Native-American game, Lacrosse.

Lacrosse is one of many stickball-type games. Early data (1630s) reports that this game was played by Native-American men throughout the eastern half of North America. French explorers named the game after the French word "crosse," meaning curved stick. Non-natives in Montreal, Canada, took up the game, created official rules, introduced it to other countries, and declared Lacrosse their national sport.

Today women and men alike enjoy this intense game. Lacrosse is very popular with secondary and college students. Lacrosse continues to draw more players each year.

These Scottish women are playing for different teams. They are wearing kilts as part of their Lacrosse uniform. One player is trying to get the ball out of the other player's "pocket." When a player puts the hard rubber ball into the opponent's net, they've scored!

Oral history

Migrants in many countries are now taking part in **oral history** projects, in which they are interviewed about their memories of the past. They describe their old culture, and the challenges of settling into a new culture. Oral history is an important way of recording migrants' experiences when they move from one country to another.

Maria Donato's family

Maria Donato was born in 1915 in a village in Italy. She arrived in Australia in 1933.

Interviewer: *What was it like at home in Ascoli Piceno?*

Maria: *We lived near a river. I would get round pebbles from the river and play knucklebones with them. I used to knit socks for the boys, help do the washing by hand, and make wine with my Dad.*

Interviewer: *What sorts of food did you have?*

Maria: *My mom and I used to make the bread. We had our own chickens, eggs, rabbits for eating, a vegetable garden, and a vineyard. We made our own sausages, and stored them for the cold winter months. We didn't have a refrigerator or ice-chest. To keep meat cool, we put it in a bag and put it down the well.*

Interviewer: *What did you learn about at school?*

Maria: *Our teacher would read to us from the newspaper. She read about Marconi's invention of the wireless. I had to leave school when I was ten, after which I learned dressmaking.*

Interviewer: *Did you have a radio ever at home?*

Maria: *We never had a radio. We listened to the news in the village where the men used to talk about politics.*

Interviewer: *What about friends?*

Maria: *All my friends were special. They were like members of my family. There was dancing when the farmers finished the harvest. There was food, too; ravioli, torte, and other sweets. Everyone went.*

Interviewer: *When did you come to Australia and why did you come?*

Maria: *When I was about ten, Dad went to live in Australia because he thought the climate would be better for his health. Dad worked so Mom and my brothers could join him. It took eight years before I saw him again. I remember his address because I was always writing to him.*

CHAPTER 10

Change in Time

Almost every culture in the world is changing today. The greatest changes come from the effects of new technology.

Modern transport has changed many cultures. Cars, buses, and trains have often replaced walking, riding horses, and cycling. People can now travel great distances in much less time.

Computers have made life very different from 100 years ago. People can travel the world on the internet and e-mail news to friends and family in distant countries at the touch of a button.

As technology allows people around the world to mix more and more, cultures will continue to change.

# Glossary

black bun   a pie-like Scottish dessert so full of raisins and currants that it looks black

ceremony   an occasion, such as a tea ceremony, wedding or graduation, when traditional activities are carried out

coat of arms   an emblem or symbol that represents a country, city, or family

emblem   a symbol

festival   a fun time when people get together to celebrate something such as a harvest, a kind of music, or an event in the past

graduation   a ceremony when someone completes a segment of education or special qualification

migrate   to move from one country to another to live

oral history   history passed down by word of mouth, often in an interview

proverb   an old saying, giving advice to others

tucker   an informal, or casual, word for everyday food

virtual traveler   a person who learns about other countries using the Internet; feeling as though they are visiting another country